THE POWER OF
DIGITAL MARKETING

Master the Art of Online Promotion
to Boost Your Business

Ray Goodwin

CONTENTS

LIABILITY DISCLAIMER

The information contained within this book is intended for informational purposes only and should not be construed as legal or professional advice. The authors and publishers of this book are not responsible for any losses or damages that may arise from the use of the information contained within.

The reader assumes full responsibility for any decisions made based on the information in this book. The authors and publishers do not endorse any particular method, service or product mentioned in this book and are not responsible for any consequences resulting from their use.

The reader should exercise caution and discretion when making life changing decisions, and should be aware of the risks and potential consequences of their actions. This book is not a substitute for professional or legal advice and should not be relied upon as such.

By reading and using the information in this book, the reader acknowledges and agrees to hold harmless the authors, publishers, and any other parties involved in the creation or distribution of this book from any and all liability, claims, damages, or losses that may arise from their use of the information contained herein.

CHAPTER 1: INTRODUCTION TO DIGITAL MARKETING

Welcome to The Power of Digital Marketing! In this book, I will guide you through the world of online marketing and show you how to maximize your business's potential in the digital age. With over 25 years of experience in online sales, I have seen firsthand the incredible benefits that come with a strong digital marketing strategy.

But what exactly is digital marketing? Simply put, it is the use of various online platforms and tactics to promote products or services. From search engine optimization (SEO) to social media advertising, there are countless ways to reach your target audience and drive conversions.

In this book, I will not only explain the different types of digital marketing but also provide practical tips on how to create a comprehensive strategy tailored specifically for your business. We will cover topics such as building a strong online presence, identifying your target audience, creating compelling content, measuring success through analytics, and much more.

Whether you are an entrepreneur just starting out or an established business looking to expand your online reach, The Power of Digital Marketing is here to help you succeed in today's digital landscape. So let's dive in and discover the power of digital marketing together!

Overview

In today's fast-paced and tech-driven world, digital marketing has become an integral part of any successful business strategy. From small start-ups to billion-dollar corporations, savvy marketers are leveraging the power of digital channels to reach their target audience and drive growth.

But what exactly is digital marketing? Simply put, digital marketing is the promotion of products or services using digital platforms such as search engines, social media, email, and mobile apps. Unlike traditional marketing, which relied heavily on print, radio, and television advertising, digital marketing allows for more targeted and personalized messaging, as well as instant feedback and tracking of campaign performance.

The Evolution of Digital Marketing

Digital marketing has seen an exponential growth in recent years. According to a report by Hootsuite and We Are Social, as of January 2021, around 4.2 billion people all over the world use the internet, and 3.8 billion are active social media users. This huge audience presents an immense opportunity for businesses to reach out to potential customers and build relationships with existing ones.

Digital marketing has come a long way since its inception in the early 1990s. In the early days, digital advertising was limited to banner ads and pop-ups, which were often seen as intrusive and annoying to users. Over the years, however, digital marketing has evolved to become more sophisticated, personalized, and engaging. With the rise of social media platforms like Facebook, Twitter, and LinkedIn, businesses can now interact with customers in real-time and create targeted campaigns based on their interests and behaviors.

Why Digital Marketing Matters

Digital marketing matters because it allows businesses to connect with their target audience in a more meaningful, relevant, and cost-effective way. Unlike traditional advertising, digital marketing allows for greater targeting, personalization, and measurement of campaign performance. It provides businesses with a wealth of data and insights that they can use to improve their marketing strategies and create more engaging content.

Another reason why digital marketing matters is that today's consumers are increasingly using digital channels to research and make purchasing decisions. According to a study by Retail Dive, 87% of shoppers now begin their search for products online. This means that businesses that fail to establish a strong digital presence run the risk of losing out on potential sales and customers.

Benefits of Digital Marketing

There are several benefits of digital marketing that businesses can take advantage of. For one, it is a cost-effective way to reach a large audience. Unlike traditional advertising, which is often expensive and has limited reach, digital marketing platforms such as social media, search engines, and email allow businesses to target specific demographics and interests at a much lower cost.

Another benefit of digital marketing is that it allows for greater engagement and interactivity with customers. Through social media platforms, businesses can create meaningful conversations with customers and build relationships built on trust and transparency. This can lead to increased loyalty and repeat business.

Challenges of Digital Marketing

While there are many benefits to digital marketing, there are also significant challenges that businesses need to be aware of. One challenge is the constantly evolving nature of digital platforms and technologies. What works today may not necessarily work tomorrow, and businesses need to stay informed of the latest trends and best practices to avoid falling behind.

Another challenge is the sheer amount of noise and competition in the digital space. With so many businesses vying for the attention of consumers, it can be difficult to stand out and create content that resonates with your target audience.

Digital Marketing Strategies

To be successful in digital marketing, businesses need to have a clear and concise strategy in place. This means defining goals and objectives, identifying target audiences, and selecting the right digital channels and tactics to reach them.

Digital marketing strategies can include a mix of paid, owned, and earned media. Paid media refers to advertising on digital platforms such as search engines, social media, and display ads. Owned media refers to the content that a business owns, such as its website, blog, and social media profiles. Earned media refers to the coverage and mentions a business receives from external sources, such as media outlets and influencers.

Types of Digital Marketing Channels

There are a variety of digital marketing channels that businesses can utilize to reach their target audience. These include:

- ❖ Search engine marketing (SEM): SEM involves paid advertising on search engines such as Google and Bing to drive traffic and conversions.

- ❖ Social media marketing: Social media marketing involves creating and sharing content on social media platforms such as Facebook, Twitter, and LinkedIn to engage with customers and drive brand awareness.

❖ Email marketing: Email marketing involves communicating with customers via email to promote products and services, nurture leads, and drive conversions.

❖ Content marketing: Content marketing involves creating and sharing valuable content such as blog posts, videos, and ebooks to attract and engage customers.

❖ Video marketing: Video marketing involves creating and sharing video content on platforms such as YouTube and Facebook to promote products and services.

Elements of Successful Digital Marketing Campaigns

Successful digital marketing campaigns share several common elements. These include:

❖ A clear and concise message that resonates with the target audience

❖ Consistent branding and messaging across all digital channels and assets

❖ A deep understanding of customer needs, pain points, and behaviors

❖ A focus on engagement and interaction with customers

❖ A data-driven approach that allows for continuous optimization and improvement

In conclusion, digital marketing has become an essential component of any successful business strategy, allowing businesses to connect with their target audience in a more meaningful and cost-effective way. While there are challenges to overcome, businesses that develop clear and concise digital marketing strategies and tactics can reap the benefits of increased customer engagement, loyalty, and sales growth.

CHAPTER 2: UNDERSTANDING YOUR AUDIENCE

In today's digital age, it is more important than ever to understand your audience. With the abundance of data available, it has become easier to gain insights into your target market's needs, preferences, and behaviors. Failing to understand your audience can be detrimental to a digital marketing campaign, leading to wasted resources and missed opportunities. In this chapter, we will explore the key elements of audience research and how to effectively gather and analyze data to inform your digital marketing strategy.

Importance of Audience Research

Audience research is the foundation of any effective digital marketing strategy. Without a clear understanding of who your target audience is, what motivates them, and how they behave online, it is impossible to create compelling campaigns that resonate with them. Audience research helps you identify the right channels to use, the right messaging to convey, and the right tactics to employ to achieve your marketing goals.

Creating Customer Personas

One of the most effective ways to understand your audience

is by creating customer personas. Customer personas are fictional representations of your ideal customers, based on data and insights gathered through research. They outline the characteristics, behaviors, and motivations of your target audience, providing a framework for your digital marketing campaign.

To create customer personas, you should start by analyzing your existing customer data. This can include demographic information, such as age, gender, income, and location, as well as behavioral data, such as browsing and purchase history, social media activity, and email engagement. From this data, you can identify common patterns and trends that help you build a picture of your ideal customer.

Once you have identified key characteristics of your target audience, you can create detailed customer personas that outline their goals, challenges, pain points, and preferences. This information can then be used to inform your marketing messaging, targeting, and content creation.

Identifying Customer Needs and Pain Points

Another important aspect of audience research is identifying customer needs and pain points. This involves understanding the challenges and problems that your target audience faces and how your products or services can address them. By addressing customer pain points, you can create messaging that resonates with your audience and positions your brand as a solution to their problems.

To identify customer needs and pain points, you can conduct market research through surveys, focus groups, or user testing. This can provide insights into your customers' opinions, preferences, and behavior patterns, helping you identify areas where your brand can add value.

Analyzing Customer Data

Data analysis is a crucial element of audience research. By analyzing customer data, you can gain insights into your audience's behavior patterns, preferences, and pain points. This can be done through various techniques, including data mining, predictive analytics, and machine learning.

Data mining involves analyzing large datasets to identify patterns and trends that can inform your marketing strategies. Predictive analytics uses statistical modeling to forecast future trends and behaviors, allowing you to make data-driven decisions. Machine learning involves training algorithms to improve their decision-making capabilities based on data analysis.

Segmentation and Targeting

Segmentation and targeting are key elements of audience research. By segmenting your audience, you can group customers based on common characteristics, such as age, location, interests, or behavior patterns. This allows you to tailor your marketing messages and content to each segment, increasing the chances of conversion.

Targeting involves identifying the most relevant segments for your brand and developing marketing strategies to attract and retain them. This can involve using targeted messaging, personalized content, and other tactics that speak directly to your target audience.

Building Relationships with Customers

Building relationships with customers is another important aspect of digital marketing. By engaging with your audience through social media, email marketing, and other channels, you can build trust and loyalty, increasing the chances of conversion and repeat business.

To build relationships with customers, you should focus on providing value and creating a two-way dialogue. This can involve educating your audience about your products or services, sharing relevant content, and responding to feedback and inquiries in a timely and personalized manner.

Measuring Customer Satisfaction

Measuring customer satisfaction is crucial to understanding your audience and improving your digital marketing strategies. This can be done through various metrics, including Net Promoter Score (NPS), Customer Satisfaction (CSAT), and Customer Effort Score (CES).

NPS measures the likelihood of customers to recommend your brand to friends or family, providing insights into how well your brand is perceived. CSAT measures customer satisfaction with specific products or services, while CES measures how easy it is for customers to use your products or services. By analyzing these metrics, you can identify areas for improvement and develop strategies to enhance customer loyalty and advocacy.

In conclusion, understanding your audience is essential to the success of your digital marketing campaigns. By conducting detailed audience research, creating customer personas, and analyzing customer data, you can develop targeted strategies that resonate with your target audience. This can lead to increased engagement, higher conversion rates, and greater brand loyalty, ultimately driving business growth and success.

CHAPTER 3: CREATING A WINNING WEBSITE

Your website is often the first point of contact that potential customers have with your business. Therefore, it is essential to have a website that is not only visually appealing but also user-friendly and optimized for SEO. In this chapter, we will discuss how to create a winning website that will attract and retain visitors, convert them into leads or customers, and help your business achieve its goals.

Website design and layout

In a world where attention spans are getting shorter and shorter, website design and layout play an integral role in the success of your website. A well-designed website should be visually appealing, easy to navigate, and provide a seamless user experience. When designing your website, it is crucial to keep in mind that less is often more. A cluttered website layout can be overwhelming for visitors and may drive them away.

Your website design should also reflect your brand's identity, including your brand colors, logos, and tone. It is essential to create a cohesive design that is consistent across all pages of your website to build brand recognition and trust.

Content strategy

Once you have a visually appealing website layout, it is time to focus on creating high-quality, valuable content that appeals to your target audience. Content is not only important for engaging visitors but also for SEO purposes. Search engines like Google prioritize websites with high-quality, relevant content, which can help improve your website's search engine ranking.

When creating your website's content, it is crucial to understand your target audience and identify their needs and pain points. You should think about the questions they might have and create content that provides answers and solutions. For example, if you run a fitness website, your audience may be interested in articles on weight loss, strength training, cardio, and nutrition. By providing valuable content that is both informative and engaging, you can build trust with your audience and increase the likelihood of converting them into customers or leads.

Website optimization for search engines

Search engine optimization, or SEO, is the process of optimizing your website to improve its visibility in search engine results pages (SERPs). When done correctly, SEO can increase website traffic, improve your website's visibility, and drive more conversions. There are two main types of SEO: on-page and off-page optimization.

On-page SEO refers to optimizing individual web pages to rank higher in search engine results and improve their relevance to specific keywords. On-page optimization includes:

❖ Adding meta-tags (title tags, meta descriptions, and header tags) to each page of your website.

❖ Optimizing your website's images by compressing image sizes, adding alt tags, and providing descriptions.

❖ Creating unique and high-quality content that provides value to visitors.

❖ Optimizing your website's URL structure so that it is easy to understand and includes relevant keywords.

Off-page SEO refers to the efforts you make outside of your website to improve your ranking on search engines. Off-page optimization includes:

❖ Building high-quality backlinks to your website from other reputable websites.

❖ Creating engaging social media content that drives traffic back to your website.

❖ Engaging with your audience on social media and building a community of followers.

❖ Generating positive online reviews and building your online reputation.

User experience and usability

User experience, or UX, plays a crucial role in the success of your website. UX is about ensuring that users can find the information they need, understand it easily, and navigate your website with ease. When designing for UX, it is crucial to keep the following in mind:

❖ Focus on page speed. Websites that load quickly are more engaging for users and are often rewarded by search engines.

❖ Create a responsive website design that is optimized for mobile devices.

❖ Use intuitive navigation that makes it easy for users to find what they are looking for.

❖ Optimize website forms and checkout pages to make it easy for users to fill out forms and complete checkouts.

❖ Test your website's usability by conducting user testing sessions and incorporating feedback from users.

Call-to-actions

A call-to-action (CTA) is a phrase or button that encourages users to take a specific action. Examples of CTAs include "subscribe now," "sign up for our newsletter," or "schedule a free consultation." CTAs are essential for converting website visitors into leads or customers, and they should be strategically placed on your website to encourage users to take action.

When creating CTAs, it is essential to make them clear, concise, and compelling. They should be easy to find, and they should provide a benefit to users. CTAs should also be tested and optimized to ensure the best conversion rates.

Mobile optimization

In today's mobile-first world, optimizing your website for mobile devices is no longer optional. With more people accessing the internet from their smartphones and tablets, having a mobile-optimized website is crucial for providing a seamless user experience. Mobile optimization includes creating a responsive website design that adapts to different screen sizes, compressing images to help pages load faster, and optimizing website forms and checkout pages to make it easier for mobile users to complete them.

Website security

Website security is crucial for protecting your business and your customers from cyber threats. Hackers can steal sensitive data, infect your website with malware or viruses, or take your website down altogether. To protect your website, it is essential to do the following:

✓   Use secure web hosting.

✓   Keep your website updated with the latest security patches and software updates.

✓   Use strong passwords and two-factor authentication.

✓   Use SSL (Secure Sockets Layer) encryption to protect data.

Analytics and tracking

Website analytics and tracking are crucial for understanding how your website is performing and making data-driven decisions to improve its performance. Analytics tools like Google Analytics can provide insights into website traffic, user behavior, and conversion rates.

By tracking key metrics like bounce rate, time on site, and conversion rates, you can identify areas for improvement and optimize your website accordingly. You can also use website tracking to monitor user behavior and see which pages of your website are most popular, which CTAs are most effective, and which content is driving the most traffic.

Conclusion

A winning website is essential for the success of your digital marketing campaign. A well-designed and optimized website can attract and retain visitors, provide a seamless user experience, and help improve your search engine rankings. By focusing on website design, content strategy, website optimization, user experience, and security, you can create a website that is not only visually appealing but also effective at driving conversions. Remember to continually test and optimize your website based on user feedback and performance metrics to ensure that it remains effective over time.

CHAPTER 4:
SEARCH ENGINE
OPTIMIZATION (SEO)

In today's digital age, search engines have become a vital tool for individuals and organizations to find information, products, and services online. Search engine optimization (SEO) is the practice of optimizing your website to improve its visibility and ranking on search engines. SEO is crucial for any digital marketing strategy, as it helps increase website traffic, generate leads, and boost revenue. In this chapter, we will explore in detail the best practices for SEO and how to measure its success.

What is SEO?

SEO refers to the process of optimizing your website to rank higher on search engines such as Google, Bing, and Yahoo. SEO involves both on-page and off-page optimization techniques to improve the quality and relevance of the content on your website. The goal of SEO is to attract organic traffic to your website through increased visibility and ranking on search engine result pages (SERPs). Search engines use complex algorithms to determine the relevance and authority of a website, and SEO is all about understanding these algorithms and optimizing your website accordingly.

Keyword Research:

Keyword research is the first and most important step in SEO. Keyword research involves identifying the keywords and phrases that people use to search for products or services related to your business. The goal is to target the keywords that have high search volume and low competition. There is a range of tools available for conducting keyword research, such as Google Keyword Planner, SEMrush, and Ahrefs.

On-page optimization:

On-page optimization involves optimizing the content and website structure to make it more search engine friendly. On-page factors that contribute to SEO include the title tag, meta description, header tags, URL, and internal linking. The goal is to create high-quality, relevant, and engaging content that is easy to read and understand for both search engines and users.

Off-page optimization:

Off-page optimization refers to the techniques used to improve your website's reputation and authority. Off-page factors that contribute to SEO include link building, social media sharing, and guest blogging. The goal is to generate high-quality backlinks from authoritative websites in your niche. Backlinks are like votes of confidence, and the more high-quality backlinks you have, the more authoritative your website appears to search engines.

Link building:

Link building is the process of getting other websites to link back to your website. The quality and relevance of the linking website are critical factors in determining the value of the backlink. Building backlinks requires a lot of time and effort, and there are many tactics and strategies available. Some of the most effective tactics include guest blogging, broken link building, and content promotion.

Local SEO:

Local SEO is essential for businesses with a physical presence such as restaurants, retail stores, and service providers. Local SEO involves optimizing your website and online presence specifically for local searches. The goal is to improve the visibility of your business in local search results and increase foot traffic to your physical location. Local SEO tactics include optimizing your Google My Business profile, building citations and NAP consistency, and getting reviews and ratings from customers.

SEO tools and metrics:

There is a wide range of SEO tools available that can help you improve your website's visibility and ranking on search engines. Some of the most popular SEO tools include Google Analytics, Google Search Console, SEMrush, Ahrefs, and Moz Pro. These tools provide valuable insights into your website's performance, such as website traffic, click-through rate, bounce rate, and conversion rate.

Measuring SEO success:

Measuring the success of your SEO efforts requires monitoring and analyzing various metrics such as organic traffic, ranking position, and website engagement. The ultimate goal of SEO is to drive traffic and conversions, and these metrics can help you determine the effectiveness of your SEO strategy. Regular monitoring and analysis of SEO metrics are essential to identifying areas for improvement and adapting your SEO strategy accordingly.

Conclusion:

SEO is an essential component of any digital marketing strategy. Optimizing your website and online presence for search engines can help you drive organic traffic, generate leads, and increase revenue. Keyword research, on-page optimization, off-page optimization, link building, local SEO, and SEO tools and metrics are all critical factors in a successful SEO strategy. By monitoring and analyzing SEO metrics, you can measure the effectiveness of your SEO efforts and make informed decisions about optimizing your website for search engines.

CHAPTER 5: PAY-PER-CLICK (PPC) ADVERTISING

PPC, also known as paid search advertising, is a form of digital marketing that allows businesses to place ads on search engine results pages (SERPs) and other websites and only pay when someone clicks on their ad. PPC is a powerful tool for driving traffic to a website and generating leads and sales. In this chapter, we'll explore the basics of PPC advertising, how it works, and how to create and optimize campaigns for maximum effectiveness.

Introduction to PPC

PPC advertising is a way to buy visits to your website rather than earning them organically through search engine optimization or other means. When someone searches for a keyword that's relevant to your business, your ad appears at the top or bottom of the search engine results page. Ads can also appear on other websites that have agreed to show ads that are relevant to their audience.

There are several PPC platforms available, but the two most popular ones are Google Ads and Facebook Ads. Google Ads is the largest and most popular platform, with over 90% of the search engine market share. Facebook Ads is a social media advertising platform that allows businesses to create and target ads to specific audiences based on demographics, interests, behaviors, and other factors.

Ad Creation and Targeting

Creating effective ads is key to running a successful PPC campaign. Ads should be relevant, compelling, and aligned with the searcher's query. You'll need to carefully choose your ad copy, headlines, and images to entice people to click on your ad.

To target your ads to the right audience, you'll need to choose the right keywords and set targeting parameters. Keywords are the words or phrases that someone might use in a search engine query to find what they're looking for. You'll need to research and select the keywords that are relevant to your business and have a high search volume.

Targeting parameters allow you to choose who can see your ads based on factors such as demographics, location, interests, and behaviors. The more targeted your ads are, the more likely they are to resonate with your audience and drive conversions.

Keyword Research and Selection

Keyword research and selection are critical to the success of your PPC campaigns. You'll need to research and select keywords that are relevant to your business, have a high search volume, and are not too competitive. Using tools like Google's Keyword Planner or SEMrush can help you find the right keywords for your ads.

Once you have a list of relevant keywords, you'll need to choose which keywords to target in your campaigns. You'll want to choose keywords that have a high search volume, are relevant to your business, and are not too competitive. You can also use negative keywords to exclude certain keywords that are not relevant to your business.

Bid Management

In a PPC campaign, businesses bid on keywords that they want to target with their ads. The amount you bid determines how much you pay when someone clicks on your ad. Bid management is the process of optimizing your bids to ensure that you're getting the most value for your money.

To optimize your bids, you'll need to monitor your campaigns closely and make adjustments as needed. You'll want to adjust your bids based on factors such as the competition for the keywords you're targeting, the performance of your ads, and your budget constraints.

Ad Performance Tracking and Optimization

Tracking and optimizing the performance of your ads is critical to getting the most out of your PPC campaigns. You'll need to monitor your campaigns closely to see what's working and what's not.

You'll want to track important metrics such as click-through rate (CTR), conversion rate, and cost per click (CPC). These metrics can help you identify which ads are performing well and which ones need improvement.

To optimize your ads, you'll need to make adjustments based on your performance metrics. You might need to tweak your ad copy, adjust your targeting parameters, or change your bidding strategy. Continuously testing and optimizing your ads is the key to achieving success with PPC advertising.

Remarketing Campaigns

Remarketing is a powerful feature of PPC advertising that allows you to target people who have already interacted with your business. For example, you can target people who have visited your website or added items to their cart but did not complete the checkout process.

Remarketing ads can be highly effective because they're targeted to people who have already shown an interest in your business. They can also be used to remind people about your brand and reinforce your message.

Measuring PPC Success

Measuring the success of your PPC campaigns is critical to understanding your ROI and making data-driven decisions. You'll need to track important metrics such as ROI, conversion rate, and cost per acquisition (CPA).

ROI is a measure of the return on investment you're getting from your PPC campaigns. It's calculated by dividing your total revenue by your total advertising costs. Conversion rate is the percentage of people who convert after clicking on your ad. CPA is the amount, you're paying to acquire each new customer.

By tracking these metrics, you can identify which campaigns are performing well and which ones need improvement. You can also use this data to make informed decisions about your bidding strategy, ad copy, and targeting parameters.

Conclusion

PPC advertising is a powerful tool for businesses of all sizes to drive traffic to their website and generate leads and sales. By creating targeted ads, choosing the right keywords, and monitoring and optimizing your campaigns, you can achieve success with PPC advertising.

In the next chapter, we'll explore social media marketing, another essential component of digital marketing. We'll discuss how to create and execute a social media strategy that engages your audience and drives conversions.

CHAPTER 6: SOCIAL MEDIA MARKETING

Social media has become an essential component of digital marketing strategies. With over 3.6 billion active social media users globally, businesses are leveraging social media platforms to engage with their target audiences, build brand trust, and increase sales. In this chapter, we'll explore the best practices and strategies for mastering social media marketing.

Social Media Platforms

There are several social media platforms that businesses can use to reach their target audience. Facebook remains the most popular platform, with 2.79 billion active users. However, businesses can also use other platforms, such as Twitter, LinkedIn, Instagram, YouTube, and TikTok.

The key to selecting the right social media platforms is understanding your target audience's preferences and behavior. For example, if your target audience is predominantly professionals, LinkedIn might be the best platform to reach them. Similarly, if your target audience is primarily teenagers and young adults, then you may want to focus on platforms like TikTok and Instagram.

Social Media Strategy

A successful social media marketing strategy requires a well-defined plan of action. Before you start creating content for social media, you need to clearly outline your goals and objectives. Some common goals of social media marketing may include increasing brand awareness, driving traffic to your website or e-commerce store, or generating leads and sales.

Once you have identified your goals, you can begin creating a content calendar that aligns with your business objectives. The content calendar should outline the types of content you will create, when you will post, and on which platform. Your content should be engaging, educational, and entertaining, while also establishing your business as a thought leader in your industry.

Building a Social Media Presence

Your social media presence is a direct reflection of your business. Therefore, it's important to make a good first impression. Consistent branding across all social media platforms is crucial to building brand recognition and trust with your target audience.

To increase your social media following, you can leverage social media advertising options, such as sponsored posts and paid social media advertisements. In addition, collaborating with influencers who have a large following can help expand your reach.

Social Media Content Creation and Curation

Creating original content is a great way to showcase your brand's personality and creativity. However, it can be time-consuming and expensive. To overcome this, you can curate content from other sources. Share links to articles or blogs that align with your brand values to offer valuable information to your followers.

Social Media Advertising

Social media advertising is an effective way to increase the visibility of your brand, target a specific audience, and drive traffic to your website. Facebook and Instagram have powerful advertising tools that allow businesses to customize their ads to reach their target audience based on demographics, location, interests, and behaviors.

In addition, Twitter and LinkedIn also provide their own advertising options tailored to the demographic and interests of their users. Advertisements can include sponsored content, banner ads, or promotional videos.

Social Media Analytics and Monitoring

To measure the effectiveness of your social media strategy, it is essential to track metrics and key performance indicators (KPIs). These metrics can include engagement rate, reach, follower count, clicks, conversions, and revenue generated from social media.

Social media monitoring tools such as Hootsuite, Sprout Social, or Buffer can help you track the success of your social media strategy by providing detailed reports on follower growth, engagement rate, and content performance.

Influencer Marketing

Influencer marketing is a popular strategy for many businesses that want to increase brand awareness and generate leads. By collaborating with influencers, businesses can leverage the influencer's large following to increase their own social media visibility and drive traffic to their website.

To find the right influencer for your business, you can use influencer marketing platforms like HypeAuditor, Scrunch, or Influencer, which can connect you with influencers who align with your brand values and target audience.

Measuring Social Media Success

To measure the success of your social media marketing efforts, you need to set specific goals and KPIs, and track these metrics over time. Your goals may include increasing brand awareness, driving traffic to your website, generating leads and sales, or building a community.

Once you have identified your goals, you can use tools like Google Analytics, social media analytics, or other marketing automation platforms to track and analyze metrics that matter most to your business. Regular monitoring and tracking will help you identify areas for improvement and adjust your strategy accordingly.

In conclusion, social media marketing can be a powerful tool for businesses to connect and engage with their target audience, increase brand awareness, and drive sales. By creating an effective social media strategy, building a strong social media presence, sharing valuable content, and leveraging social media advertising options, businesses can gain a competitive edge in an increasingly digital world.

CHAPTER 7: EMAIL MARKETING

Email marketing is often overlooked in today's digital landscape, with many businesses focusing their marketing efforts on social media and PPC advertising. However, email marketing remains a valuable and effective tool for businesses of all sizes.

Introduction to email marketing:

Email marketing is the act of sending targeted marketing messages to a group of people through email. These messages can include newsletters, promotional offers, and other types of content. Email marketing is one of the oldest forms of digital marketing and is still one of the most effective.

Building a subscriber list:

The first step in a successful email marketing campaign is building a subscriber list. This list should include people who have given you permission to contact them via email. You can build your list by offering sign-up forms on your website, social media platforms, or in-store, and incentivizing people to sign up.

Email design and templates:

Once you have your subscriber list, it's time to create visually appealing emails with engaging content. This starts with email design and templates. The design of your email should be consistent with your brand and include eye-catching images, clean layouts, and easy-to-read font.

Email content strategy:

The content of your email is also critical to your success. The content should be relevant and valuable to your subscribers, engaging, and easy to read. The type of content you include in your emails can vary from newsletters to promotional offers, event invitations, exclusive content, and more.

Personalization and segmentation:

Personalization is key to a successful email marketing campaign. Personalized emails get opened more often, and subscribers appreciate the personal touch. Segmentation is also important, as it allows you to send targeted messages to specific groups within your subscriber list.

Email automation:

Automation is another critical component of a successful email marketing campaign. Automation allows you to send targeted emails to your subscribers based on their behavior, interests, and other criteria.

Deliverability and testing:

Once you've created your email and segmented your list, it's time to send it out. However, before you do, you must ensure that your email is delivered successfully. This means testing your email, checking for spam triggers, and optimizing your email for deliverability.

Measuring email marketing success:

Finally, you must measure the success of your email marketing campaign. This involves tracking your open rates, click-through rates, and conversion rates. You can also use A/B testing and other techniques to optimize your email marketing campaigns for better results.

Conclusion:

Email marketing is a highly effective way to engage with your audience and drive sales. By building a subscriber list, creating engaging content, personalizing your emails, implementing automation, optimizing for deliverability, and measuring your success, you can create a successful email marketing campaign that will help you build better relationships with your customers and increase revenue.

CHAPTER 8: CONTENT MARKETING

Content marketing has become an essential aspect of digital marketing. It is a powerful way to communicate and engage with potential customers. However, it is not just about creating any content. The focus should be on creating high-quality content that resonates with your target audience and delivers value to them.

What is Content Marketing?

Content marketing is the process of creating valuable and relevant content to attract, engage, and retain a clearly defined audience. The content could be in any format, including blog posts, videos, podcasts, infographics, social media posts, and more.

The idea behind content marketing is to build trust and relationships with potential customers by providing them with useful and informative content. By doing so, you are positioning yourself and your brand as a thought leader and a trusted source of information.

Content Creation and Planning

Before creating any content, it is essential to identify the target audience and understand their needs and pain points. You can use customer personas created in Chapter 2 to determine the kind of content that would interest them.

Creating a content plan helps establish a clear direction for the content strategy. It should consider the platform, the format, and the topics that the brand wants to cover. The plan should be flexible and allow for spontaneous ideas to be included.

Content Distribution and Promotion

Creating excellent content is only the first step. It needs to be distributed to the target audience effectively. The distribution channels could vary according to the format of the content.

For written content, it could be disseminated via blog posts, email newsletters, and social media. For videos, YouTube and other video hosting platforms could be used, and for infographics, social media platforms such as Instagram, Pinterest, and Twitter can be effective in promoting the content.

Using email marketing campaigns is another way to distribute and promote new content to subscribers, providing a direct link to the latest blog posts, podcasts, or videos that are relevant to them. Social media can be used to share snippets of new content with a call-to-action to visit the website to read more.

Content Optimization for Search Engines

Optimizing content for search engines is an essential aspect of content marketing. It helps in generating organic traffic, increasing visibility, and attracting more visitors to the website.

The optimization process involves identifying the keywords and phrases that potential customers would use in search engines. Tools such as Google Keyword Planner can assist in this step. Once the keywords are identified, they should be subtly integrated into the content, including the headlines, meta tags, and the body of the content.

Storytelling in Content Marketing

Storytelling is a powerful tool that can be used to communicate complex ideas and engage people emotionally. It is an effective way to capture the attention of potential customers and keep them engaged with the content.

Storytelling can be achieved through different forms of content, including blog posts, videos, and infographics. The key is to create a narrative that resonates with the target audience, highlighting the solutions that the brand offers.

Interactive Content Types

Interactive content types, such as quizzes, polls, and infographics, can be effective in engaging the target audience. By asking questions, the content can become more personalized to the reader, leading to higher engagement.

Interactive content types can also offer unique insights into the customers' attitudes and opinions, further helping to refine the content plan.

Building a Brand Through Content Marketing

Content marketing can effectively contribute to building a brand. By establishing the brand as a thought leader in the industry and providing valuable content, it can attract potential customers and retain existing ones.

The content should be aligned with the brand's values and reflect the company's identity. It should also be consistent in tone, style, and messaging.

Conclusion

Content marketing is a powerful tool in the digital marketer's toolkit, allowing brands to communicate with potential customers and engage with them in meaningful ways. However, to be successful with content marketing, it requires a clear understanding of the target audience, content creation and planning, content distribution and promotion, optimization, and storytelling. By creating valuable and engaging content, brands can establish trust and relationships with potential customers and grow their businesses.

CHAPTER 9: VIDEO MARKETING

Video marketing has become increasingly crucial in today's digital marketing strategies. It provides an eye-catching and engaging way to showcase products, services, and brand stories. Videos are also versatile in their format and can be used across various platforms, making them a must-have tool for any digital marketer. In this chapter, you will learn about the importance of video marketing, types of video content, video creation tools and resources, video distribution and promotion, video optimization for search engines, video advertising options, measuring video marketing success, and best practices for video marketing.

Importance of Video Marketing

There are many reasons why video marketing has become essential in today's digital marketing landscape. A recent study shows that video marketing content generates 1200% more shares than text and images combined. Videos have also been shown to increase conversions, user engagement, and brand loyalty. Video content is a powerful storytelling tool that can evoke emotions, memories, and inspire action in ways that text and images cannot match.

Types of Video Content

There are various types of video content that digital marketers should consider when developing video marketing campaigns.

Explainer videos, product demos, how-to videos, brand stories, customer testimonials, and behind-the-scenes videos are just a few examples. Each type of video content can serve specific marketing goals. For example, explainer videos can help educate potential customers about a new product or service, while customer testimonials can increase brand credibility and trust.

Video Creation Tools and Resources

Creating professional-quality videos does not require a Hollywood budget. There are many video creation tools and resources available online that can help digital marketers create video content. Software solutions such as Adobe Premiere Pro, Final Cut Pro, and iMovie can be used to edit professional-grade videos, while platforms such as Canva, Wave.video, and Animoto provide drag-and-drop templates for creating eye-catching and engaging videos without any technical skills. Stock footage websites such as Shutterstock and Getty Images can also be used to find high-quality video footage to include in your video marketing campaigns.

Video Distribution and Promotion

Once you have created your video marketing content, the next step is getting it in front of your target audience. You can distribute your videos through various channels such as YouTube, Facebook, Instagram, and LinkedIn. Each platform serves a different purpose, and it is crucial to understand how to optimize your video content for each platform to maximize engagement. Video length, format, and aspect ratio are just a few factors to consider when publishing your video content on various platforms.

Video Optimization for Search Engines

Optimizing your video content for search engines is called

Video Search Engine Optimization (VSEO). Proper VSEO can help your video content rank higher in search engine results pages, increasing visibility, and engagement. VSEO includes optimizing video titles, descriptions, tags, and transcripts. Including relevant keywords in your video content and using closed captions can also improve your video's SEO.

Video Advertising Options

Video advertising is an effective way to increase brand awareness and drive conversions. Platforms such as YouTube, Facebook, and TikTok offer various video advertising options such as pre-roll ads, skippable ads, and promoted videos. Each type of video advertising serves a different purpose and can be optimized depending on your target audience and marketing goals.

Measuring Video Marketing Success

Measuring the success of your video marketing campaigns is essential to understand what is working and not working. Various metrics can be used to track the performance of your video content. Metrics such as views, engagement, click-through rates, and conversion rates are just a few of the many KPIs that should be tracked to determine the success of your video marketing campaigns.

Best Practices for Video Marketing

To maximize the impact of your video marketing campaigns, here are some best practices to consider:

- ❖ Keep it Short and Engaging - The ideal length for videos is 2-3 minutes. Ensure that the video content is engaging and captivating from the start to keep the audience engaged.

- ❖ Optimize for Mobile - The majority of videos are consumed on mobile devices. Ensure that your videos are optimized for mobile viewing, and the format is compatible with various mobile devices.

❖ Add a Call-to-Action - Add a clear Call-to-Action at the end of the video to encourage viewers to take action.

❖ Brand Continuity - Ensure that your video content aligns with your brand's tone, messaging, and design.

❖ Experiment - Experiment with different video content types, distribution channels, and advertising options to determine what works best for your brand.

Conclusion

In conclusion, video marketing has become a crucial component of any digital marketing strategy. With the right planning, resources, and execution, video marketing can help increase engagement, conversions, and brand loyalty. Understanding the different types of video content, video creation tools and resources, video distribution and promotion, video optimization for search engines, video advertising options, measuring video marketing success, and best practices for video marketing can help digital marketers create compelling and effective video marketing campaigns.

CHAPTER 10: MOBILE MARKETING

Mobile marketing has become one of the most important digital marketing channels in recent years. With the increasing use of smartphones and tablets, marketers can no longer ignore mobile users. In this chapter, we will discuss the different mobile marketing strategies, channels, and best practices that you can use to reach your target audience on their mobile devices.

Introduction to Mobile Marketing

Mobile marketing involves reaching your target audience through their smartphones and tablets. The aim is to deliver personalized and relevant messages at the right time and place. Mobile marketing allows you to engage with your customers in real-time, across multiple platforms, and devices.

In-App Advertising

In-app advertising involves placing ads within mobile apps. This can be done in various formats, like banner ads, video ads, native ads, and interstitial ads. In-app advertising is an effective way to reach your target audience, as users spend most of their time in apps. The key is to ensure that the ads are relevant to the app content and the user's interests.

SMS Marketing

SMS marketing involves sending text messages to your customers' mobile phones. This is a great way to reach your target audience, as almost everyone uses messaging apps. The key to SMS marketing is to ensure that your messages are personalized, relevant, and timely. You should also provide users with an easy way to opt-out of receiving messages.

Mobile Websites and Apps

Mobile websites and apps are two different mobile marketing channels. A mobile website is a responsive website that can be accessed from any mobile device. A mobile app, on the other hand, is a downloadable application that can be installed on a mobile device. Both mobile websites and apps provide users with easy access to your products and services and allow you to engage with them in real-time.

Push Notifications

Push notifications are messages that are sent to your customers' mobile devices, even when they are not using your app. These notifications can be used to encourage users to open your app, make a purchase, or take other actions. It's important to ensure that your notifications are personalized, relevant, and timely.

Location-based Marketing

Location-based marketing involves using a user's location data to deliver personalized and relevant messages. This can be done through geofencing, which involves setting up a virtual perimeter around a physical location, and sending messages to users who enter or exit that area. Location-based marketing is an effective way to target users based on their location, interests, and behaviors.

Mobile Analytics and Tracking

Mobile analytics and tracking involve monitoring and analyzing user behavior on your mobile website or app. This allows you to understand how users are interacting with your mobile content and make data-driven decisions to improve their experience. Mobile tracking can help you identify user pain points, track user acquisition and retention, and measure user engagement.

Measuring Mobile Marketing Success

Measuring mobile marketing success involves tracking key performance indicators (KPIs) like app downloads, app engagement, click-through rates, conversion rates, and ROI. The key is to ensure that you are measuring the right metrics and using them to make data-driven decisions. It's important to remember that mobile marketing is a constantly evolving landscape, so the metrics you track today may not be relevant tomorrow.

Best Practices for Mobile Marketing

To ensure that your mobile marketing campaigns are successful, you need to follow some best practices. These include optimizing your mobile content for speed and usability, ensuring that your messages are personalized and relevant, tracking user behavior and responding in real-time, and testing different strategies to identify what works best. It's also important to keep up-to-date with the latest mobile marketing trends, technologies, and regulations.

Conclusion

Mobile marketing is an essential part of any digital marketing strategy. With the increasing use of smartphones and tablets, marketers can no longer ignore mobile users. To succeed in mobile marketing, you need to deliver personalized and relevant messages at the right time and place, optimize your mobile content for speed and usability, and track user behavior in real-time. By following these best practices, you can reach your target audience on their mobile devices and achieve your digital marketing goals.

CHAPTER 11:
AFFILIATE MARKETING

Affiliate marketing is a performance-based marketing strategy where an affiliate earns a commission for promoting a company's products or services. With affiliate marketing, companies can expand their reach and increase sales while affiliates can earn a passive income by promoting relevant products or services to their audience.

What is Affiliate Marketing?

Affiliate marketing is a revenue-sharing model where a company pays commissions to affiliates who promote their products or services, and drive sales or leads to the company's website. The affiliate is usually an individual or a company, who has an audience or a customer base that may be interested in the company's products or services. The affiliate promotes the company's products or services through various channels, such as their website, blog, social media, email marketing, and so on.

Affiliate Marketing Programs and Networks

To set up an affiliate marketing program, the company can either create an in-house affiliate program or join an affiliate network. In-house affiliate programs are managed by the company itself, and they provide affiliates with unique tracking links or codes to use when promoting the company's products or services. The company can set its own commission rates and pay affiliates directly.

On the other hand, affiliate networks are third-party platforms that connect companies with affiliates and manage the affiliate program on behalf of the company. In an affiliate network, the company provides the products or services, and the network provides the platform, tracking, payment processing, and support for affiliates. The network charges a fee or a commission for its services.

Affiliate Recruitment and Management

To attract affiliates, companies need to create a compelling offer that motivates them to promote the company's products or services. This offer can include commission rates, cookie duration, product information, promotional materials, support, and so on. Companies can also use affiliate directories, social media, email marketing, and affiliate forums to reach potential affiliates.

Once affiliates have joined the program, companies need to provide them with the necessary tools and resources to promote the products or services effectively. These resources can include banners, text links, videos, landing pages, product reviews, and promotions. Companies can also provide affiliates with training, support, and feedback to help them improve their performance.

Commission Structures and Payouts

Commission rates vary depending on the industry, competition, and product type. Some companies offer a percentage of the sale, while others offer a flat fee per lead or per click. The cookie duration is another factor that companies need to consider when designing their affiliate program. The cookie is a piece of tracking code that allows companies to track the affiliate's referrals for a certain period after the initial visit. The longer the cookie duration, the higher the chances of conversion, but also the higher the risk of commission fraud.

Affiliate tracking and reporting are essential for measuring the success of the program and calculating commissions. Companies can use tracking software, such as Google Analytics, or affiliate network tools to track clicks, leads, and sales attributed to the affiliates. Payouts can be made through various channels, such as PayPal, wire transfer, or check, depending on the affiliate's preferences.

Best Practices for Affiliate Marketing

To run a successful affiliate marketing program, companies need to follow some best practices:

❖ Choose the right affiliates: Focus on quality, not quantity. Select affiliates who have a relevant audience and a good reputation in the industry.

❖ Provide valuable resources: Give affiliates the tools and resources they need to promote the products or services effectively. Make it easy for them to share their links and track their referrals.

❖ Set realistic goals: Define clear goals and benchmarks for the program and communicate them to the affiliates. Reward affiliates for achieving these goals.

❖ Monitor and optimize: Monitor the performance of the program and the affiliates regularly. Identify areas for improvement and optimize the program accordingly.

Measuring Affiliate Marketing Success

To measure the success of the affiliate marketing program, companies should track the following metrics:

❖ Click-through rate (CTR): The percentage of clicks on the affiliate's link compared to the impressions or views.

❖ Conversion rate (CR): The percentage of visitors who complete the desired action, such as making a purchase or filling out a form.

❖ Average order value (AOV): The average amount of money that a customer spends per transaction.

❖ Cost per acquisition (CPA): The cost of acquiring a customer through the affiliate marketing program.

❖ Return on investment (ROI): The profit earned from the affiliate marketing program compared to the investment made.

Future of Affiliate Marketing

Affiliate marketing has been around for decades and has evolved with the digital age. The future of affiliate marketing is expected to be driven by technology, automation, and personalization.

Automation will enable companies to streamline their affiliate marketing programs and reduce the manual effort required to manage them. This will include automating the recruiting, tracking, payment, and reporting processes.

Personalization will allow companies to offer customized products or services to their customers and tailor their affiliate offers to their specific needs and preferences. This will involve using artificial intelligence, machine learning, and customer data to create targeted promotions and recommendations.

The future of affiliate marketing will also be influenced by the changing regulations and privacy concerns. Companies will need to comply with data protection laws, such as GDPR and CCPA, and adhere to ethical standards in their marketing practices.

Affiliate marketing is a powerful strategy that allows companies to expand their reach, increase sales, and build relationships with their affiliates and customers. By following the best practices and measuring the success of the program, companies can leverage affiliate marketing to achieve their business goals and stay ahead of the competition.

CHAPTER 12: ANALYTICS AND DATA VISUALIZATION IN DIGITAL MARKETING

In today's digital world, data has become a key ingredient in the recipe for success in digital marketing. The ability to analyze and interpret data can help businesses make informed decisions, identify opportunities for growth, and measure the effectiveness of their marketing campaigns. In this chapter, we'll explore the importance of analytics and data visualization in digital marketing, and how businesses can leverage them to improve their marketing efforts.

Importance of Data in Digital Marketing

Data is the lifeblood of any digital marketing campaign. It provides a wealth of information about your audience, their interests, behaviors, and preferences, and enables you to make informed decisions about your marketing strategy. Data can reveal insights that you may not have even considered, allowing you to identify areas of opportunity that might have otherwise gone unnoticed.

However, data is only useful if you know how to use it. In digital marketing, there is often an overwhelming amount of data available, which can be challenging to manage and analyze. That's why it's essential to have a clear understanding of what you want to achieve with your data and how you plan to use it.

Web Analytics Tools

Web analytics tools are designed to help businesses track and measure their website's performance. They provide valuable insights into how visitors are interacting with your site, the pages they are visiting, how long they stay, and where they are coming from.

Google Analytics is one of the most popular web analytics tools. It's a free tool that offers a comprehensive suite of features that enable you to track and analyze key metrics related to your website's performance. Some of the essential metrics that Google Analytics provides include:

❖ Traffic sources: This metric tells you where your website visitors are coming from, such as search engines, social media platforms, or referral sites.

❖ Pageviews: This metric tells you how many pages on your website were viewed by visitors.

❖ Bounce rate: This metric tells you the percentage of visitors that left your website after viewing only one page.

❖ Conversion rate: This metric tells you the percentage of visitors that completed a desired action, such as making a purchase or filling out a contact form.

Other popular web analytics tools include Adobe Analytics, Piwik, and Clicky.

Key Performance Indicators (KPIs) in Digital Marketing

Key performance indicators (KPIs) are specific metrics that businesses use to measure the success of their marketing campaigns. KPIs can vary depending on the business objectives, but they should be closely aligned with the goals of the campaign. Here are some examples of KPIs that businesses commonly use in digital marketing:

❖ Website Traffic: Number of unique visitors, page views, bounce rate, and session duration

❖ Lead Generation: Number of leads, conversion rate, cost per lead, and lead quality

❖ Sales: Revenue, conversion rate, average order value, and customer lifetime value

❖ Social Media: Reach, engagement, follower growth, and click-through rates

❖ Email Marketing: Open rate, click-through rate, conversion rate, and unsubscribe rate

Data Visualization Best Practices

Data visualization is the art of presenting data in a graphical format that is easy to understand. It allows businesses to communicate complex data in a visual way, enabling stakeholders to make informed decisions quickly. Here are some best practices for creating effective data visualizations:

❖ Choose the right format: Different types of data lend themselves to different visual formats, so it's essential to choose the right format for the data you have.

❖ Keep it simple: Avoid cluttering your visualization with unnecessary details or distracting elements. The goal is to make it easy to understand at a glance.

❖ Select the right colors: The choice of colors can impact the readability and effectiveness of your visualization. Use color to highlight important data and to create contrast.

❖ Use annotations and labels: Annotations and labels can provide additional context to your visualization, making it easier to understand.

❖ Tell a Story: A good data visualization should tell a story, highlighting the most important insights and enabling stakeholders to make informed decisions.

Dashboards and Reporting

Dashboards and reporting tools allow businesses to monitor their marketing performance in real-time. They enable stakeholders to visualize key metrics and KPIs, identify trends, and track progress towards achieving their goals. Some popular dashboard and reporting tools include:

❖ Google Data Studio: Data Studio provides a comprehensive suite of data visualization and reporting tools that enable businesses to create custom dashboards that are easy to share and update.

❖ Tableau: Tableau is a powerful data visualization tool that enables businesses to create interactive dashboards that provide real-time insights into their marketing performance.

❖ Databox: Databox is a reporting tool that enables businesses to visualize key metrics and KPIs from multiple sources in a single dashboard.

A/B Testing and Experimentation

A/B testing or split testing is a method used to test different variations of a marketing campaign to determine which one performs better. In A/B testing, two versions of a campaign are created, with one element changed in the second version. The results are then compared to determine which version performs better.

A/B testing can be used to test anything from the subject line of an email to the design of a webpage. Experimentation is similar to A/B testing, but with more variables being tested simultaneously. Experimentation is an excellent way to test multiple variations of a campaign and optimize for the best-performing version.

Conversion Rate Optimization

Conversion rate optimization (CRO) is the process of optimizing a website or marketing campaign to increase the percentage of visitors that take a desired action, such as making a purchase or filling out a form. CRO involves analyzing data to identify areas of the campaign that can be improved, such as the copy, design, or call-to-action.

CRO is essential because it enables businesses to get the most out of their existing traffic. By optimizing their marketing campaigns, businesses can increase their conversion rates without having to spend additional money on advertising.

Measuring ROI in Digital Marketing

Measuring the return on investment (ROI) of a marketing campaign is vital for businesses to determine the effectiveness of their marketing efforts. To calculate ROI, businesses must track the costs associated with the campaign and the revenue generated as a result of the campaign. Here are some essential metrics businesses can use to measure the ROI of their digital marketing campaigns:

- ❖ Cost per acquisition (CPA): The amount of money it costs a business to acquire a new customer.

- ❖ Customer lifetime value (CLV): The total amount of revenue a business can expect to generate from a customer over the life of their relationship with the business.

❖ Return on ad spend (ROAS): The revenue generated by a campaign divided by the cost of the campaign.

❖ Return on investment (ROI): The revenue generated by a campaign minus the cost of the campaign, divided by the cost of the campaign.

Conclusion

Analytics and data visualization are essential components of digital marketing. By understanding how to collect, analyze, and visualize data, businesses can make informed decisions about their marketing strategies and identify areas of opportunity for growth. By using the right tools and KPIs, businesses can measure the effectiveness of their marketing campaigns, optimize for better results, and increase their ROI. In the next chapter, we'll explore marketing automation, which is another critical component of digital marketing.

CHAPTER 13: MARKETING AUTOMATION

In today's fast-paced world, digital marketing has become an indispensable part of any business. As businesses expand, so does the need for efficient and effective marketing strategies. In recent years, marketing automation has emerged as one of the most critical tools in the digital marketer's arsenal. Marketing automation refers to the use of software to automate repetitive marketing tasks with the goal of streamlining workflows and increasing efficiency.

Marketing automation offers numerous benefits to businesses of all sizes and industries. Some of these benefits include increased lead generation, improved lead conversion rates, better customer engagement, increased revenue, and improved customer satisfaction. In this chapter, we'll discuss the benefits of marketing automation and how to set it up for maximum effectiveness.

Benefits of marketing automation

Marketing automation offers several benefits to digital marketers. First, it enables marketers to create and deliver personalized, targeted content that resonates with their audience. By leveraging data and analytics, marketers can segment their audience and deliver highly personalized messages to each group.

Second, it helps marketers streamline workflows and automate repetitive tasks. For example, marketers can automate email campaigns, follow-up emails, lead scoring, and lead nurturing. This frees up valuable time and resources that marketers can use to focus on more strategic initiatives.

Third, marketing automation helps improve lead generation and conversion rates by nurturing leads and running targeted campaigns to keep leads engaged and moving through the sales funnel. With marketing automation, businesses can ensure that leads are not lost in the pipeline and that they are progressing towards conversion.

Finally, marketing automation helps improve customer satisfaction by engaging with customers at the right time with the right message. By delivering timely, relevant information, marketers can build stronger relationships with customers and keep them engaged with the brand.

Marketing automation tools and platforms

Marketing automation tools and platforms vary in scope and complexity. Some tools focus on specific marketing functions, while others offer end-to-end solutions that cover multiple marketing channels. Here are some of the most popular marketing automation tools and platforms:

❖ Hubspot - Hubspot is an all-in-one marketing and sales platform that includes email marketing, social media management, lead management, and analytics. It offers a drag-and-drop interface and a range of pre-built templates, making it easy for marketers to create and launch campaigns.

❖ Marketo - Marketo is a comprehensive marketing automation platform that offers lead management, email marketing, social media marketing, mobile marketing, and analytics. It features a drag-and-drop interface and advanced reporting and analytics capabilities.

❖ Eloqua - Eloqua is a top-rated marketing automation platform that offers a range of features, including lead nurturing, email marketing, website tracking, and social media management. It also provides advanced analytics and reporting capabilities.

❖ Pardot - Pardot is a marketing automation platform that is best suited for B2B companies. It offers email marketing, lead management, lead scoring, and ROI reporting.

❖ ActiveCampaign - ActiveCampaign is a comprehensive marketing automation platform that offers email marketing, CRM, lead management, and eCommerce capabilities. It features an intuitive drag-and-drop interface and advanced automation workflows.

Automated email campaigns

Email marketing is a critical component of any marketing automation strategy. Automated email campaigns enable marketers to engage with customers and leads at the right time with the right message. Here are some of the most common types of automated email campaigns:

❖ Welcome emails - Welcome emails are sent to new subscribers or customers to introduce them to the brand and provide information about products or services. They can also be used to offer a discount code or other incentive to encourage a first purchase.

❖ Abandoned cart emails - Abandoned cart emails are sent to customers who have added items to their cart but haven't completed the purchase. These emails can be used to remind customers of their abandoned cart, offer a discount code, or provide additional recommendations.

❖ Follow-up emails - Follow-up emails are sent to customers or leads who have engaged with the brand but haven't converted. These emails can be used to provide additional information about products or services, address customer concerns, or offer incentives to convert.

❖ Customer retention emails - Customer retention emails are sent to existing customers to encourage repeat purchases, provide new product or service information, or offer loyalty rewards.

Lead nurturing and scoring

Lead nurturing and scoring are critical components of any marketing automation strategy. Lead nurturing involves building relationships with leads over time by providing relevant, personalized content through various channels. Lead scoring refers to the process of assigning a value to a lead based on their behavior and engagement with the brand. Here are some best practices for lead nurturing and scoring:

❖ Segment your audience - Segment your audience based on demographics, behavior, interests, or lifecycle stage. This enables you to deliver targeted content that resonates with each group.

❖ Offer value - Provide valuable, educational content that addresses customer needs and pain points. This builds trust and credibility with your audience and encourages them to engage with your brand.

❖ Use multi-channel touchpoints - Use a combination of channels (email, social media, website, etc.) to engage with your audience and deliver your message.

❖ Use lead scoring - Assign scores to leads based on their behavior, engagement, and demographics. This enables you to prioritize leads and focus your resources on those with the highest potential to convert.

Workflow automation

Workflow automation involves automating repetitive marketing tasks to streamline workflows and increase efficiency. This includes tasks such as lead routing, email campaigns, lead scoring, and lead nurturing. Here are some best practices for workflow automation:

- ❖ Map out your workflows - Map out your workflows and identify areas where automation can be used to streamline tasks and improve efficiency.

- ❖ Use triggered actions - Use triggered actions to automatically send emails to leads based on their behavior or status in the sales funnel.

- ❖ Use conditional logic - Use conditional logic to personalize the customer experience and deliver targeted content based on specific customer actions or preferences.

- ❖ Monitor and adjust workflows - Monitor your workflows and adjust them as needed to improve their effectiveness and efficiency.

Personalization with marketing automation

Personalization is a critical component of any marketing automation strategy. Personalized content resonates with customers and builds trust and loyalty. Here are some ways to personalize your marketing automation efforts:

- ❖ Use customer data - Use customer data (demographics, behavior, interests) to personalize your content and messaging.

- ❖ Use dynamic content - Use dynamic content to deliver personalized content based on the customer's lifecycle stage or behavior.

❖ Use personalization tokens - Use personalization tokens to insert the customer's name or other personal information into your content.

Measuring success with marketing automation

Measuring success with marketing automation involves setting goals, tracking metrics, and making data-driven decisions. Here are some of the most important metrics to track:

❖ Conversion rates - Measure the percentage of leads that convert to customers.

❖ Customer lifetime value - Measure the total value of a customer over the course of their relationship with the brand.

❖ Click-through rates - Measure the percentage of subscribers or leads who click on your emails or ads.

❖ Open rates - Measure the percentage of subscribers or leads who open your emails.

❖ ROI - Measure the return on investment for your marketing automation efforts.

In conclusion, marketing automation is a powerful tool that enables businesses to streamline workflows, increase efficiency, improve lead generation and conversion rates, and build stronger relationships with customers. With the right tools and strategies, marketing automation can help businesses of all sizes and industries thrive in the digital age.

CHAPTER 14: CUSTOMER RELATIONSHIP MANAGEMENT (CRM)

In this chapter, we will explore the concept of Customer Relationship Management (CRM) and its significance in digital marketing. We will also discuss how companies can leverage CRM to build a stronger relationship with their customers and drive business growth.

What is CRM?

CRM is a strategy that businesses use to manage interactions with customers throughout the customer lifecycle. It is an approach that puts the customer at the center of the strategy and aims to build long-term relationships with them. CRM involves collecting and analyzing customer data, which helps companies understand their customers better and cater to their needs effectively.

Benefits of CRM

CRM has numerous benefits, including:

❖ Enhancing customer experience: By understanding customers' needs and preferences through their data, companies can offer personalized experiences that meet their expectations.

❖   Improving customer retention: CRM enables companies to build strong relationships with their customers, making it more likely that they will continue to do business with them.

❖   Increasing efficiency: By automating repetitive tasks such as data entry and analysis, companies can increase efficiency and improve productivity.

❖   Enabling collaboration: CRM systems enable cross-functional teams to work together, allowing for better coordination and communication, leading to more effective customer management.

CRM Platforms and Tools

There are numerous CRM platforms and tools available in the market, such as:

❖   Salesforce: Salesforce is one of the most popular CRM platforms used by companies worldwide. It offers a range of features such as lead management, marketing automation, and sales forecasting.

❖   HubSpot: HubSpot is an all-in-one marketing, sales, and service platform that offers CRM features alongside other tools. The platform is suited for small and mid-sized businesses.

❖   Zoho CRM: Zoho CRM is a cloud-based platform that offers features such as lead and contact management, social media integration, and workflow automation.

❖   Microsoft Dynamics 365: Microsoft Dynamics 365 is a cloud-based CRM platform that offers features such as sales and marketing automation, customer service, and project management.

Customer Data Management

One of the key components of CRM is the management of customer data. Companies must collect and manage customer data effectively to ensure that they can provide personalized experiences. Some of the key elements of effective data management are:

❖ Data collection: Companies must collect comprehensive data from various sources such as their website, social media, and point of sale systems. This data must be accurate and up-to-date.

❖ Data cleaning: Data must be cleaned and standardized to prevent errors and inconsistencies.

❖ Data warehousing: Data must be stored securely in a centralized system, making it easier to access and analyze.

❖ Data analysis: Companies must analyze customer data to gain insights into their behavior and preferences. This enables them to create targeted marketing campaigns, identify trends, and make informed business decisions.

Lead Management and Nurturing

CRM enables companies to manage leads effectively, from initial contact to conversion. By using lead scoring and nurturing techniques, companies can focus their efforts on the most promising leads, increasing the likelihood of a sale.

Sales Pipeline Management

CRM enables companies to manage their sales pipeline effectively, tracking deals from initial contact to closure. By using pipeline management techniques such as sales forecasting, sales teams can prioritize their efforts and improve win rates.

Marketing and Sales Alignment

CRM enables better alignment between marketing and sales teams. By using data analytics and tracking, both teams can access real-time data, enabling them to collaborate on campaigns and coordinate efforts more effectively.

Measuring Success with CRM

CRM success can be measured using key performance indicators such as customer satisfaction scores, customer retention rates, and sales win rates. Companies can also analyze the effectiveness of their CRM strategy by tracking metrics such as lead conversion rates and customer acquisition costs.

In conclusion, CRM is an essential component of a comprehensive digital marketing strategy. By using CRM platforms and tools, companies can manage customer data effectively, build strong relationships with their customers, and drive business growth. Effective CRM enables companies to provide a personalized experience to each customer, enhancing their satisfaction and increasing retention rates.

CHAPTER 15: ARTIFICIAL INTELLIGENCE (AI) AND MACHINE LEARNING IN DIGITAL MARKETING

Artificial intelligence (AI) and machine learning have become buzzwords in the world of digital marketing. AI refers to the simulation of human intelligence in machines, allowing them to perform tasks that usually require human intelligence. Machine learning is a subset of AI that allows machines to learn from data and improve their performance without being explicitly programmed.

AI and machine learning have the potential to revolutionize digital marketing by making it more efficient, personalized, and effective. In this chapter, we will explore the use cases for AI and machine learning in digital marketing, the benefits they offer, and how to measure success with AI and machine learning.

Use Cases for AI in Digital Marketing

There are several use cases for AI in digital marketing:

❖ Predictive Analytics: Predictive analytics involves analyzing historical data to predict future outcomes. AI-powered predictive analytics can help digital marketers better understand customer behavior, predict customer churn, and identify upsell and cross-sell opportunities.

❖ Chatbots and Virtual Assistants: Chatbots and virtual assistants are AI-powered tools that can answer customer queries, offer recommendations, and provide customer support. They can save time and improve customer experience by responding to customer queries immediately, 24/7.

❖ Personalization: AI can help digital marketers personalize content and experiences for each customer. By analyzing customer data, AI can provide personalized product recommendations, customize email marketing campaigns, and more.

❖ Automated content creation: AI can create and curate content, saving time and resources. For example, AI-powered tools can write product descriptions, generate social media posts, and even create video content.

Benefits of AI in Digital Marketing

The benefits of AI in digital marketing include:

❖ Efficiency: AI can automate tasks and processes, allowing digital marketers to focus on high-value activities such as strategy development and analysis.

❖ Personalization: AI can provide personalized experiences for each customer, improving customer engagement and loyalty.

❖ Insights: AI can analyze vast amounts of data and provide actionable insights, helping digital marketers make informed decisions.

❖ Accuracy: AI-powered tools can analyze data more accurately than humans, reducing errors and improving decision-making.

Measuring Success with AI and Machine Learning

Measuring success with AI and machine learning involves defining goals, selecting metrics, and analyzing data. Here are some metrics to consider:

❖ Conversion Rates: Measure the percentage of visitors who take a desired action, such as making a purchase or requesting more information.

❖ Engagement: Measure how often users interact with your brand across different channels.

❖ Customer Satisfaction: Monitor customer feedback to understand their satisfaction with your brand and identify areas for improvement.

❖ Cost Savings: Measure the cost savings achieved by automating tasks and processes using AI.

❖ ROI: Measure the return on investment from using AI in digital marketing.

Future of AI in Digital Marketing

The future of AI in digital marketing looks promising. As AI continues to evolve and become more sophisticated, it will enable digital marketers to provide even more personalized experiences for their customers. Additionally, AI-powered tools will become more accessible and affordable, making them available to businesses of all sizes.

However, there are also concerns about the ethical implications of using AI in digital marketing. It's important to ensure that AI is used ethically and transparently and that customers are informed about how their data is being collected and used.

In conclusion, AI and machine learning have the potential to transform digital marketing by improving efficiency, personalization, and effectiveness. As the technology continues to evolve, it's essential for digital marketers to keep up with the latest trends and best practices to stay ahead of the competition.

CHAPTER 16:
ETHICS AND DIGITAL MARKETING

As the world becomes increasingly digitized, the marketing industry has evolved along with it. The power of data, automation, and personalization has made digital marketing more effective than ever before. However, this new power also comes with a new set of ethical considerations. In this chapter, we will explore the ethical challenges that come with digital marketing and how to address them.

Ethical considerations in digital marketing

One of the biggest ethical concerns in digital marketing is the issue of privacy. As customer data becomes more readily available, companies have a responsibility to ensure that this information is used ethically and transparently. This means that companies must be clear about what data they are collecting, how this data will be used, and who will have access to it.

Another important ethical consideration is the use of personalization. Personalization can greatly improve the customer experience, but it can also be perceived as invasive or creepy if not done in the right way. Companies must be careful to balance personalized marketing with respect for the customer's privacy and choice.

Finally, digital marketers must be careful not to exploit vulnerable groups or perpetuate harmful stereotypes. This means being mindful of cultural sensitivities and avoiding language or imagery that may be offensive or exclusionary.

Privacy concerns and regulations

The issue of privacy has become more pressing with the introduction of data privacy regulations such as the General Data Protection Regulation (GDPR) and the California Consumer Privacy Act (CCPA). These regulations aim to give consumers more control over their personal data and protect them from misuse. Companies that fail to comply with these regulations risk facing fines and damage to their reputation.

In order to comply with these regulations, companies must be transparent about the data they collect, how it is used, and who has access to it. They must also give customers the ability to opt-out of data collection and provide a clear process for how they can do so.

Social responsibility in digital marketing

Another important aspect of ethical digital marketing is social responsibility. Companies have a responsibility to ensure that their marketing does not harm society or perpetuate harmful stereotypes. This means avoiding language or imagery that could be considered discriminatory or offensive.

In addition, companies should use their marketing to promote positive social change. For example, a company could use its platform to promote environmental sustainability or social justice causes. By aligning their marketing with social responsibility, companies can build trust with their customers and strengthen their brand.

Transparency and disclosure

One of the keys to ethical digital marketing is transparency. Companies must be transparent about their data collection and use practices, as well as any partnerships or sponsorships that may influence their marketing.

In addition, digital marketers must be clear about what they are selling and avoid misleading or deceptive tactics. This means avoiding clickbait headlines or exaggerated claims and clearly disclosing the terms and conditions of any offers or promotions.

Balancing business objectives and customer needs

Finally, digital marketers must be careful to balance their business objectives with the needs of their customers. This means avoiding tactics that may be detrimental to the customer experience or cause harm to society, even if they may be profitable in the short term.

Ethical decision-making frameworks

In order to make ethical decisions in digital marketing, companies can use frameworks such as the Ethical Framework for Digital Marketing or the Ethical Decision-Making Framework. These frameworks provide a step-by-step process for evaluating ethical issues and making decisions that align with the company's values.

Measuring ethical success in digital marketing

Measuring the success of ethical digital marketing can be challenging, as it is often difficult to quantify the impact of social responsibility initiatives or transparency measures. However, companies can track metrics such as customer satisfaction, brand reputation, and employee engagement to evaluate the success of their ethical efforts.

Best practices for ethical digital marketing

The following are some best practices for ethical digital marketing:

- ❖ Be transparent about data collection and use practices

- ❖ Balance personalized marketing with respect for privacy

- ❖ Avoid language or imagery that could be considered discriminatory or offensive

- ❖ Use marketing to promote positive social change

- ❖ Avoid deceptive or misleading tactics

- ❖ Balance business objectives with customer needs

- ❖ Use ethical decision-making frameworks to guide decision-making

Conclusion

Digital marketing has the power to drive business success, but it also comes with a responsibility to use this power ethically and responsibly. By prioritizing transparency, social responsibility, and customer needs, companies can build trust with their customers and strengthen their brand.

CHAPTER 17: GLOBAL DIGITAL MARKETING

As digital marketing continues to grow and evolve, businesses are presented with an increasing number of opportunities to expand their reach and connect with customers around the world. However, global digital marketing comes with its own set of unique challenges, including the need to navigate different cultures and languages, as well as differences in technology and infrastructure.

In this chapter, we will explore some of the challenges and opportunities of global digital marketing and discuss strategies for successfully expanding your business into new markets.

Challenges and Opportunities in Global Digital Marketing

One of the biggest challenges of global digital marketing is navigating cultural differences. What works in one market may not work in another, and cultural nuances must be taken into account when creating marketing messages, designing websites, and engaging with customers. For example, the way that a product is marketed in the United States may not resonate with consumers in China, who may have different preferences and values.

Another challenge is differences in language and translation. In order to effectively reach audiences in different countries, businesses need to be able to communicate in local languages.

This not only includes website content and marketing messages, but also customer service and support.

Despite these challenges, global digital marketing also presents a number of opportunities for businesses that are looking to expand their reach. With the ability to connect with customers all over the world, businesses can tap into new markets and grow their customer base.

Localization and Translation Strategies

In order to be successful in global digital marketing, businesses need to be able to effectively communicate with their target audience in local languages. This requires more than just translation; it also requires an understanding of cultural nuances and local preferences.

One strategy for localization is to work with local experts who can help with translation and cultural adaptation. This could include hiring a local marketing agency or working with freelance translators who are native speakers of the language and can help ensure that marketing messages are appropriately localized.

In addition to language localization, businesses also need to consider localizing their content in other ways, such as adapting website design and user experience to local preferences. For example, in Japan and other Asian countries, it is common for websites to feature a lot of white space and minimalist design, whereas in the United States, websites tend to be more cluttered and visual.

Global SEO and PPC Tactics

Search engine optimization (SEO) and pay-per-click (PPC) advertising are important strategies for driving traffic and generating leads in global markets. However, different countries may have different search engines and social media platforms that are more popular than others, which means businesses need to adapt their SEO and PPC strategies accordingly.

One approach is to work with local search engine optimization and PPC experts who have a deep understanding of the local market and can help with keyword research and targeting. This can help ensure that businesses are using keywords and targeting options that resonate with local audiences.

Cross-Cultural Content Marketing

Content marketing is an important strategy for engaging with customers around the world. However, in order to be effective in different markets, businesses need to create content that is tailored to local audiences and reflective of local cultural nuances.

One approach is to create content that is truly global in nature, such as industry news or trends that are relevant across markets. Another approach is to create content that is localized for specific audiences, such as by featuring local experts or influencers, or by creating content that speaks to specific cultural values or preferences.

Social Media Strategy Across Borders

Social media is a powerful tool for connecting with customers and building brand awareness, but it can also present a number of challenges for businesses that are looking to expand into new markets. Different countries and cultures may have different social media platforms that are popular, and businesses need to adapt their social media strategies accordingly.

One approach is to work with local social media experts who can help businesses navigate the local landscape and develop social media strategies that resonate with local audiences. This could include creating content that is tailored to specific cultural preferences or using social media influencers to help build brand awareness.

Measuring Success in Global Digital Marketing

Measuring the success of global digital marketing campaigns can be challenging, especially when different markets have different metrics and ways of measuring success. However, it is important to establish clear goals and metrics for each market, and to track progress over time.

One approach is to use analytics tools that allow businesses to track website traffic, engagement, and conversion rates across different markets. This can help businesses identify trends and make data-driven decisions about their marketing strategies.

Future of Global Digital Marketing

As digital marketing continues to evolve, businesses that are able to successfully navigate the complexities of global markets will be well positioned to capture new customers and grow their businesses. However, this will require a deep understanding of local cultures and preferences, as well as a willingness to adapt and evolve with the changing landscape of global digital marketing.

Conclusion

Global digital marketing presents both challenges and opportunities for businesses that are looking to expand their reach and connect with customers around the world. By focusing on strategies such as localization, tailored content marketing, and targeted SEO and PPC campaigns, businesses can successfully navigate the complexities of global markets and reach new audiences. With careful planning, attention to local cultures, and a commitment to measuring success, businesses can take advantage of the tremendous opportunities presented by global digital marketing.

CHAPTER 18: DIGITAL MARKETING CAREERS AND SKILLS

Digital marketing is a rapidly growing field, with new jobs and specialties emerging all the time. If you're interested in a career in digital marketing, there are several essential skills you'll need to master, as well as different career paths you can pursue. In this chapter, we'll explore some of the most in-demand digital marketing skills and careers, as well as the education and training you'll need to succeed.

Digital Marketing Skills

To succeed in digital marketing, there are several critical skills and competencies you'll need to master including:

❖ Data Analysis: As digital marketing campaigns generate large amounts of data, being able to collect and analyze that data is crucial. Understanding data collection and analysis techniques form a significant part of your skill set.

❖ SEO and PPC: Two of the most critical pillars of digital marketing are Search Engine Optimization (SEO) and Pay-Per-Click (PPC) advertising. The ability to optimize and manage campaigns on various search engines such as Google, Bing search, and social media platforms such as Facebook is fundamental.

❖ Content Marketing: Being able to create and manage a content marketing strategy, including producing engaging, high-quality content, is an essential part of digital marketing and a skill you'll need to develop.

❖ Email Marketing: Build and execute email campaigns, including sequence or automations, focusing on best practices to keep customers engaged over time is a significant skill.

❖ Social Media Marketing: With an emphasis on social media channels, crafting relevant content, and tactical promotion plan is essential.

❖ Marketing Automation: The ability to automate parts of the marketing pipeline, manage and maintain CRM data is becoming more and more necessary for digital marketers.

❖ Analytics: Collecting and analyzing marketing performance data, visualizing it in a way that resonates, drawing insights, then carry out specific tests and experiments is fundamental.

Digital Marketing Careers

Digital marketing can be a rewarding career with excellent job prospects and salaries. Here are some of the most sought-after digital marketing careers today:

❖ Marketing Coordinator: This entry-level position is responsible for performing administrative tasks to support marketing initiatives.

❖ SEO and PPC Specialist: Optimization and managing of SEO and PPC campaigns day-to-day is the primary responsibility. A high degree of technical know-how and data analysis skills will be fundamental aspects.

❖ Social Media Manager: The key focus is to handle and

manage social media handles such as Facebook, Instagram, and Twitter every day and to interact with the customers and audience in a way that effectively promotes the brand.

❖ Content Marketing Manager: Developing the content marketing strategy, producing and promoting content output is the responsibility of a Content Marketing Manager.

❖ Email Marketing Manager: The key responsibility is to manage and maintain email marketing, including newsletter, sequence, campaigns, and promotional email programs.

❖ Marketing Automation Analyst: Managing and optimizing the marketing automation pipeline, including the CRM, Email, Social Media, and other digital channels.

❖ Analytics Manager: Collecting and analyzing the marketing performance data, visualize it in a way that resonates, drawing insights, then carry out specific tests and experiments.

Digital Marketing Education and Training

Fortunately, there are plenty of educational and training opportunities available to help you learn and develop the skills you'll need to succeed in digital marketing. Here are some of the options available:

❖ Self-taught: Reading blogs, articles, online courses, and watching online tutorial videos, such as on YouTube, are great ways to learn the basics and become an expert in any of the designated areas.

❖ Industry Certifications: Many organizations unique to the digital marketing industry such as Google, Hubspot, and Hootsuite offer certifications. Completing these certifications enhances the resume and demonstrates your understanding of any given digital marketing specialty.

❖ College Degrees: Pursuing college degrees in the areas of marketing, communications, or data sciences leads to foundational and advanced knowledge, opening up doors for many opportunities within the field.

❖ Digital Marketing Bootcamps and Workshops: These programs will put you on a fast-track learning path on any of the given digital marketing specialties in a matter of weeks.

Conclusion

Digital marketing is an ever-evolving field, with new technologies and techniques emerging all the time. By honing your skills and staying on top of industry trends, you can become a valuable member of the digital marketing community. Pursuing a career in digital marketing will keep you up-to-date with technological and social progressions that shape the future of society. With the right skills and experience in hand, you can make a meaningful impact for any business or client.

CHAPTER 19: CASE STUDIES AND SUCCESS STORIES

In this chapter, we will explore real-life examples of successful digital marketing campaigns across various industries, and the lessons we can learn from them.

Case Study 1: Nike

Nike is one of the most successful companies when it comes to digital marketing. In 2018, they launched the "Dream Crazy" campaign featuring Colin Kaepernick, which was designed to promote Nike's new line of athletic wear. The campaign was designed to appeal to younger, socially-engaged consumers who are passionate about social issues. The ad received both praise and backlash, but it ultimately resulted in a 31% increase in sales and a 6% increase in stock price.

Lessons Learned:

- ❖ Taking a stance on social issues can be a powerful way to connect with consumers who share your values.

- ❖ Controversial ads can be effective when executed carefully and authentically.

Case Study 2: Airbnb

Airbnb is an online marketplace that allows homeowners to rent out their homes to travelers. In 2017, they launched a digital campaign called "We Accept" that highlighted the company's commitment to diversity. The campaign featured a video that showcased Airbnb hosts who were refugees, people of color, and members of the LGBTQ+ community. The ad was highly successful, earning over 20 million views on YouTube, and resulted in a 20% increase in bookings.

Lessons Learned:

❖ Authentically showcasing your company values can resonate with consumers who share those values.

❖ Highlighting diverse perspectives can appeal to a wide range of consumers.

Case Study 3: Dollar Shave Club

Dollar Shave Club is an online retailer that sells shaving products and other grooming items. In 2012, they launched a digital campaign that featured a humorous video showcasing the company's unique value proposition and brand personality. The video went viral, and within 48 hours, the company had received 12,000 orders. The campaign was so successful that the company was acquired by Unilever for $1 billion in 2016.

Lessons Learned:

❖ A unique brand personality can help you stand out in a crowded market.

❖ Humor can be a powerful tool for engagement.

Case Study 4: Trello

Trello is a project management tool that allows teams to collaborate online. In 2017, they launched a digital campaign called "Power-Ups" that highlighted the platform's unique features and capabilities. The campaign included a series of humorous videos that showcased different use cases for Trello. The videos were highly successful, resulting in a 48% increase in sign-ups and a 33% increase in conversions.

Lessons Learned:

❖   Highlighting unique features and use cases can help potential customers see the value of your product or service.

❖   Humor can be a powerful tool for engagement.

Case Study 5: Spotify

Spotify is a music streaming service that uses a data-driven approach to personalize the user experience. In 2015, they launched a digital campaign called "Year in Music" that highlighted each user's listening habits over the course of the year. The campaign included personalized playlists, infographics, and other data-driven content. The campaign was highly successful, resulting in a 50% increase in user engagement.

Lessons Learned:

❖   Personalization can be a powerful tool for engagement.

❖   Using data to create content can help bring context and relevance to your messaging.

Conclusion:

These case studies highlight some of the key elements of successful digital marketing campaigns: authenticity, humor, personalization, and unique value propositions. However, it's important to note that these campaigns were successful because they were executed in a way that was authentic and relevant to their target audience.

As digital marketing continues to evolve, it's important to stay attuned to emerging trends and changing consumer behaviors. By leveraging data and using digital tools to tell compelling stories, brands can connect with consumers on a deeper level and ultimately drive business results.

CHAPTER 20: CONCLUSION AND FUTURE OF DIGITAL MARKETING

As we come to the end of this book, we have covered a lot of ground in the ever-evolving landscape of digital marketing. From the basics of creating an effective website to the advanced techniques of marketing automation and artificial intelligence, we have explored the many strategies and channels involved in a successful digital marketing campaign.

We have seen that digital marketing is not just a tool for promoting products and services, but a means of creating meaningful relationships with customers and understanding their needs. In order to succeed in the digital age, businesses must continually adapt to new technology and consumer behavior, while upholding ethical responsibilities in their marketing practices.

Looking ahead, the future of digital marketing holds many challenges and opportunities. One major trend is the increasing importance of mobile marketing, given that the majority of internet traffic now comes from mobile devices. Brands will need to focus on optimizing their content and campaigns for mobile devices to stay ahead of the competition.

Another area of growth is the integration of artificial intelligence and machine learning in digital marketing. AI technologies can help analyze and predict customer behavior, personalize content, and automate marketing campaigns. As these technologies become more accessible, smaller businesses will also be able to take advantage of these tools and compete with larger brands.

Lastly, the importance of data in digital marketing will only continue to grow. With advancements in data visualization and analytics, businesses will be able to gain deeper insights into customer behavior, measure the success of their marketing campaigns, and make data-driven decisions to improve their strategies.

In the midst of these changes and advancements, it is important for digital marketers to stay current and adaptable. By continuously learning and experimenting, marketers can stay ahead of the curve and deliver compelling campaigns that resonate with their audience.

In conclusion, the power of digital marketing is undeniable. Its ability to reach a global audience, personalize messaging, and measure success is unparalleled. As we move forward into the digital age, the potential for growth and innovation in digital marketing is limitless. It is up to each and every one of us to embrace these changes, continue learning, and make the most of the opportunities ahead.

Final Thoughts

I hope you have gained valuable insight into the world of digital marketing. The power of this field is immense, and it only continues to grow with new technologies and innovations. Whether you are a business owner looking to improve your online presence or a marketer trying to stay ahead of the game, digital marketing can be a game-changer.

Remember, the key to successful digital marketing is not just about mastering the latest tools and techniques but also about understanding your target audience and their needs. Keep your message clear, concise and engaging while always being authentic and transparent.

As you move forward in your own journey, keep in mind that there are no shortcuts or overnight successes in this field. It takes time, patience, and hard work to build a strong online presence, but the rewards are worth it.

I want to thank you for joining me on this journey and I hope that you have found inspiration from the stories and strategies shared within these pages. Now go out there and make your mark on the ever-expanding world of digital marketing!

ABOUT THE AUTHOR

Ray Goodwin

Ray Goodwin, is the author behind this series of captivating books on Business Development and self improvement, and has left an indelible mark on the field. He was born and raised in the bustling city of London, where he developed a strong work ethic and an insatiable curiosity about the inner workings of successful businesses. Throughout his illustrious career, Ray leveraged his extensive knowledge and experience to help numerous companies flourish and prosper.

His keen insights and innovative strategies has earned him recognition, driving him to share his expertise with others. Ray believes in the power of sharing knowledge to elevate businesses and empower aspiring entrepreneurs.

Ray's dedication to his craft is evident in the numerous books he has authored on business development and self improvement. His writing style seamlessly blends practical advice, thought-provoking concepts, and real-life case studies, making his books invaluable resources for business professionals and novices alike. His ability to distill complex concepts into accessible language has greatly impacted the lives and careers of countless individuals.

Now retired from the corporate world, Ray and his beloved wife have settled in the idyllic English countryside. Surrounded by the beauty of nature, Ray finds inspiration for his writing and indulges in his hobbies.

Ray Goodwin's books continue to serve as enduring guides for those seeking success in the business world. With a wealth of experience and a deep understanding of the inner workings of businesses, Ray's work remains a testament to his passion for sharing knowledge and helping others flourish.